ONLINE PROFIT
SECRETS

HOW TO CREATE MULTIPLE STREAMS OF INCOME AND NEVER BE BROKE AGAIN!

ERIKA NINO

Copyright © 2017 by Erika Nino

All rights reserved. No part of this book may be reproduced, distributed, or transmitted in any form or by any means, including photocopying, recording, or other electronic or mechanical methods, without the prior written permission of the publisher/author, except in the case of brief quotations embodied in critical reviews and certain other noncommercial uses permitted by copyright law. For permission requests, contact the publisher/author at Erika@theprofitchic.om or visit www.theprofitchic.com for the current contact information.

ISBN: 978-1-5471-0875-6

Ordering Information:
Quantity sales. Special discounts are available on quantity purchases by corporations, associations, and others. For details, contact the publisher/author at the email address above.

Printed in the United States of America.

DEDICATION

This book is dedicated to my amazing and incredible husband, Michael M. Nino, and our son Kole Michael Nino. I am grateful for your support. May the good Lord continue to bless your lives and always give you a Psalm 91 protection!

Contents

Introduction 7

CHAPTER 1   Affiliate Marketing 19

CHAPTER 2   Blogging 31

CHAPTER 3   E-Books 41

CHAPTER 4   Creating A Course 55

CHAPTER 5   Email Marketing 65

Acknowledgements 85
About the Author 89
Resources 93
Disclaimer 95
Credits 97

Introduction

I remember back around 2005, I had decided I wanted to start selling online. So, I ordered a course that would teach me how to sell on eBay. Don't take me wrong; I did read the entire course! I even highlighted a lot of the information, LOL. I love highlighting! But like so many other people, I never took the next step to actually get started. I guess I got what you call Paralysis by Analysis.

So, instead I gave up on it. I got overwhelmed with all the information, and I started living life by default and never really pursued what I REALLY wanted to do.

The title of this book is Online Profit SECRETS. And it is not necessary because it is not a "secret". But it may as well be, because uncovering all the different ways to make money online makes it seems like it is.

Now here we are now, and the internet has exploded. And I believe it is still in its infancy. There is so much opportunity out there, that it is mind blowing, and it can be overwhelming. The Social Media movement has forever changed the way we communicate, how we meet people and how we do business, especially online. It has created many millionaires and many jobs. Have you seen all these young people creating a six-figure income online?

So, once again I have found myself with the desire to pursue what I always wanted to do in the past. I found myself at a crossroads in my life. And this time, because of the circumstances I found myself in; I came to the decision that this time, I was going to do what I had always wanted to do in the past! I have spent many years attending webinars, reading books, buying courses, etc. But where do I start?

Maybe you too have found yourself wanting to make extra money. Maybe those extra $500.00 or $1,000.00 dollars a month would completely change your life! Or perhaps you have bigger dreams and goals. Maybe you want to create a six-figure income! Maybe you hate your job! (As I did the last one I had.) Or maybe, just like me, you see yourself traveling, catching some rays in a beach resort somewhere in the world, and still making money while you are out there relaxing? Maybe your goal is to create an empire. Perhaps you already have a business (a brick-and-mortar business), but you haven't capitalized on all the possibilities and options you have to grow your business online. Maybe you are a little old-school, and you haven't changed with the times. Whatever those goals are for you, the possibilities are endless.

Actually, it was by chance that I

found myself here again. A friend of mine had told me about this phone app that I could use to grow my business. In case you were wondering which app it was and if you can use it to grow whatever business you have, you can check it out here: **www.theprofitchic.com/osp** I thought, *"With all the possibilities that existed with this app, I can promote any and as many businesses that I want."* So I fell in love with it! And of course being "The Profit Chic" that I am, I thought, *I would definitely recommend this to my friends, so why not become an Affiliate of the company?* And so I did.

OK, so now I knew that I wanted to generate income online, but where should I start? So I decided to look into the different options that are out there.

What are other people doing, and which one was the right fit for me? I wish I could have found something out there, or even a book, that could have guided me. But instead I had to research and research, and did I say research? LOL. What were the options? There are several ideas or ways or should I say a million ideas out there, but I decided to go with the main way a lot of successful people out there are doing it. Let me share with you how this book came to be.

One day I decided to go to a local networking event to meet some people and promote my affiliate business on how to grow your business and generate leads for any type of business. It's always important to get out there and meet people and build relationships. That day, I almost changed my mind about attending because I was running a little late!

That was the day I met Randrick Chance. I knew the moment I met him that we would be working together, because what he was doing in his business complemented what I was doing in mine, and we could help each other out.

Never in my wildest dreams did I imagine what other doors of opportunity that encounter would open. It is because of him that this book came to be. Through his course, mentorship, and help, I have published this book. And with his coaching, I will be creating courses to help other people with their businesses. Not only that, but because of that partnership, the opportunity came to speak at seminars, and we are also working on creating new seminars to help clients with their businesses.

When he approached me about doing a book, I thought, *"What could I possibly write about?* And then, I had an Aha moment. I said to myself, *I could share my journey about the different ways to make money online, something that I wish I had when I was first starting."*

I could write a book where I could explain and give some examples of some of the main options that are out there. Something that could give you a starting point of several different ways that you could make money online, whether it is starting from scratch, or expanding your own business. This is not a get-rich-quick thing! So, if that is your mindset, you might as well stop reading now! Although a significant amount of money has been made by some people, it will all depend on your effort and your dedication, your willingness to learn and persevere!

This book is really for people that are just starting off, and that don't know where to start!

It is my desire that it will motivate you and inspire you to take a good look at your talents and explore the possibilities of creating a better life and improve your financial situation. At least that was the case for me. If that seems to be the case for you, it's my deepest hope that you succeed. I don't know about you, but I desire to NEVER BE BROKE AGAIN!

May some of the information you find here inspire you to create the life of your dreams and the life that you truly desire. Which is the life you truly deserve!

To your Success,

Erika Nino

HERE ARE FIVE GREAT WAYS TO MAKE MONEY ONLINE

1. Affiliate Marketing

2. Blogging

3. Creating a Course

4. E-Books

5. Email Marketing

CHAPTER ONE
AFFILIATE MARKETING

What is Affiliate Marketing? Basically it is a joint venture. You would partner up with a company that owns a product. Usually you can sign up for free to represent these companies' products. There are many good companies like these affiliate market places: Clickbank, JVzoo, and Deal

Guardian, just to name a few. These companies represent different vendors that market their products through them. There are many products in different niche markets. For example, some of the topics can be on Health, Relationships, Internet Marketing, etc. The products listed through these companies are usually digital products and courses. I like digital products because they are easy to download, instead of having to ship out a product.

The commissions on some of these products can be anywhere between 50% - 75%, depending on the vendor. Now, some of the stores that we usually purchase from like Amazon, Best Buy, and Walmart just to mention a few, also have affiliate programs where you can refer customers to them through your own link, and they will pay you a commission. However, their commissions are a lot less. They start somewhere around 4%.

You make money with these types of affiliate programs by advertising these links through your website, Facebook Fan page, Blogs, etc.

You need to identify your niche market, that segment of people that would best be suited for your product. More than likely they would be interested in what you have to offer.

I like DIGITAL ENTREPRENEURS. And the reason I do is because this niche market (affiliate marketers, network marketers, e-commerce, etc.), this group of people, are open minded. They already know that online marketing works. They are into personal development, and you don't have to take them by the hand.

There are DOs and DONTs in the industry, like **spamming** (the sending of multiple unsolicited e-mails or text messages, usually for marketing). Just make sure to learn the rules and be ethical. And don't buy from your own affiliate links. Make sure you read all the rules of every particular Affiliate program.

After you have signed up to become an affiliate, you have to develop a marketing campaign to market your products and put them in front of the right customers. Remember, it's not just because you build it that "they will come" Get yourself a good tool to help you create Opt-In pages and Sales Funnels. There are a lot of good and simple tools out there that you can use. Don't worry. You don't have to be an expert and know code or anything like that. Believe me, if I can do it, anyone can! If you can copy, paste and type, you can do this! This is why I like this particular one.

I love the fact that with this particular software, once you create some of these Sales Funnels you can make money from your phone and your computer. This is the one I use: www.theprofitchic.com/osp. They make it so easy to build the pages and funnels. Actually, there are many different templates you can use depending on your niche.

You can change the background picture, the colors, the fonts, etc. But what I love the most is that I can create as many sales funnels as I want. And once I have built my funnel, and connected it to my own autoresponder, which (is a software that you use for email automation) it will notify me in real time on my phone which makes a cool "CHA CHING" sound (like the sound a cash register makes when you sell something) to let me know someone is interested in my offer. That makes it super-easy to follow up with the prospect, when the lead is HOT. If you would like to take a closer look on what this software does, I will share the link here, so you can take a closer look at the details.

As a matter of fact, this is what

got me started in Affiliate marketing. I got this software to help me promote my husbands' business and my own. Then I realize how it could help so many other business owners that I decided to become an affiliate of the company. You can take a closer look here, www.theprofitchic.com/ospaffilliate . If you don't have a business of your own yet, no worries; you can always become an affiliate for this product and earn a residual commission every month.

BRAND BUILDING

Once you decide on the product or niche you will be going into, this is where the FUN really begins! You need to build your brand and your following. Using different types of Social Media and other methods, you can create a following. You want to do this to build trust with your audience. Why do you want to do this? Because people will buy from people they trust! I believe it was Zig Ziglar that said,

"If people like you, they'll listen to you, but if they trust you, they'll do business with you."

So, the more content you create, the more you educate, and the more you empower your niche market the bigger your audience will grow.

However, although posting on Social Media and empowering your audience and educating them will add value to them, and that will help you grow your following, that still isn't enough to make you money online; so you are going to need some tools to help you boost your brand and your profits.

You will need to do some email marketing campaigns to reach your prospects with your offers. I will be covering more on email marketing in the next chapter.

Let me give you a little analogy here: you would not try to build something with your bare hands, right? You would need some tools!

Same thing here when you are building your online business. You will be needing some tools that would help you build your business.

After you have decided which niche market you wish to serve or which product you want to sell online, no matter what opportunity in this book you want to follow, you will be needing the following:

#1 And the most important one is having a POSITIVE MINDSET. You don't want to sabotage yourself with a negative mindset.

#2 SALES FUNNEL Software. This will help you create your offers and capture leads (potential customers).

#3 Software that can help you with AUTOMATED FOLLOW-UP.

#4 BACK END PRODUCTS (these are several different price-point products that you can offer your prospect). I will be covering more detail on creating some Sales Funnels that you can implement to any niche and market on the Email Marketing chapter.

CHAPTER TWO
BLOGGING

Another way to make money online is blogging. What is blogging? Basically, it's a form of website where you can pick a topic on something that you are passionate about. You can write articles on that topic to share with your readers about the subject. You can take the expertise that you have on the subject and write about it. It can even be about cooking your favorite recipes. Maybe it's about health and staying in shape, or perhaps it's about starting a business.

Since there are a lot of blogs out there, take some time to visit other blogs in your niche. Research your market to identify what makes your blog different from the most popular blogs that are out there to help it stand out! This would make a huge difference, and it could accelerate your blog's growth.

Create a spreadsheet to start your research on your competition. Find out what they are writing about. Analyze to see if there are gaps in the areas of what they are writing about that maybe you can fill in to make your blog different?

Here is a resource you can use: **Moz.com**. This tool ranks websites and pages of websites out of 100. This way you can get an idea who your competitors are and where your blog website ranks in comparison to theirs. Check Google also to find other tools like this, since the web is constantly changing.

There are different companies that can host your blog. Two of the most popular ones are **Wordpress.org** or **Wordpress.com**. One of these is free; the other one you pay for. There are pros and cons to having one versus the other. For more details on how their services work, please visit their web sites and look into the details.

Build relationships with other bloggers.
Participate on their blogs by leaving comments on their posts. Network with them, just as you would if you went to a networking event. Bloggers like to collaborate with other bloggers. But it's all about building relationships. The internet makes it so easy, everyone is just a click away!

Once you have built your audience (and that will depend on how well you write your copy) your readership will start to increase. At this point you can start promoting some product that you can sell or should I say, *recommend* to your readers.

For example:

Monetizing your Blog

You can write your own eBook, or you can promote someone else's book that is relevant to your topic, which can pay you a commission of about 50%. You can go to **Clickbank** to find a book. If the book you are selling from the Affiliate is well received, you can sell other products from that same affiliate, like a course or audio CDs.

You can also start selling advertising on your blog. You could charge anywhere from $50.00 to $100.00 a month to put their banners on your blog. These can be sponsors from niches that correlate with yours.

You can grow your income as well by starting a newsletter for your blog. They say, "The money is in your email list" once you have a list of people, you can email them offers as well (more details on email marketing in another chapter). There's also a science to this, but if done effectively it can be very profitable.

One very important key, is that you OWN YOUR OWN blog. What that means is that you host it on your own server with your own domain name. That way you can control it.

Here is a good free Word Press resource site for beginners. If you want to start a blog, this is a good source to go to when you are starting off. This site will provide you with quality tips, hacks, tools and WordPress resources.

They have easy-to-understand tutorials for bloggers, small businesses and for people that are non-tech-savvy.

Making your marketing efforts more efficient basically boils down to three things: Content, Relationships and Technology. By creating good content, you will attract an audience. In return you will create a social following and more traffic to your site.

TOOLS: Here is a list of Providers to automate your marketing:

- MailChimp, Constant Contact, Infusionsoft, Ontraport, GetResponse, and many others.

- **Similarweb.com – This** tool you can use as a hack. Once you have discovered who your competition is and what the name of their website is, you can go to this site, type in their web addresses, and it will tell you where they are advertising, and where they are generating most of their traffic from. You can model after their marketing. If you model what is working, don't you think you will have the same success?

- **Google URL Builder** – You can add information to your URL (Web address) in Google Analytics to keep track of your links.

- **Simplymeasured.com** – A tool to analyze social media

IMAGES: Here are some tools, if you have the need to create some visuals for your social media and blog post.

- **Canva** – Create, edit, and download unique images for various things on the web (including social media posts and ads) all for free.

- **Pixabay** – This is one of my favorite Apps for images. Just type in the search button of the related image you are looking for, and you can download and use royalty free, for the exception of a few popular images that you would have to pay for if you want them.

- **Phonto** – This app I also enjoy using. I can put text on my favorite images, and use them to promote on social media.

Or, if you choose, you can use your own photos. You can upload them from your computer, Facebook, or Google Drive.

CHAPTER THREE
CREATING A COURSE

Creating your own course and selling it online is another way to generate some online income. To do this does not require professional certifications. The only qualifications you will need is your knowledge and experience. Yes, you can actually turn your skill into CASH.

The value of the online education market continues to rise. So much so, that it is projected to hit the billion dollar mark by 2022.

I recently met a young woman who is a therapist in a school, and she wants to expand her business. She has years of experience doing this. We spoke about how she could help so many people at the same time, by creating different courses and helping many people at the same time. It would be amazing to be able to help as many people as possible and in this case globally and not just locally. She is only one person, and she can only help so many people in one day. With these courses, she would be leveraging her time and resources. She could create courses on each particular issue that she currently helps her clients with. At this point since she has been doing this for so many years, she already has all the needed content, and all she has to do is start putting it in a format. In my opinion, video and some modules would probably work great for her. She should also create a sales funnel where she can have some lower price point training items, mid-size price point trainings and some highest point services. This could include a one-on-one coaching session for those clients that need a more in-depth help on a one-on-one basis.

The awesomeness about creating a course is that you do the work one time, and you can get paid multiple times for your work. Imagine creating a short course about teaching people how to do a particular task. Let's say you sell this course to 10 people for $37. You can earn $370 – or by selling it to 100 people, you would earn $3,700 and so forth and so on. These price ranges are more for smaller courses. There are courses out there in the thousands of dollars' price range. With those you would only need to sell a few a year to make a six figure income a year.

What Type of Course?

There are all types of courses out there. It can be a video course, it can be a list, and it can be in a PDF format. It can also be an audio course. I have gotten all these different types of courses; I have bought them ever since I can remember. I remember the very first course I bought to this day. It was a Tony Robbins course and it was audio. I believe I still have it. I can't see myself getting rid of it ever, lol. If you decide to do a video course, it is recommended, that you not do it that long. I actually have a course on marketing on Instagram. What I really liked about it is that the information is given to you in bite size pieces. Mind you, there are quite a few small videos in that course, but to me it makes it so much easier to learn and apply. And it does not feel overwhelming to learn. Every video is a point into that particular subject.

Beta Testing Your Course

Yes, it can be a challenge and take some time and money, but the good news is, you can start earning money, before you even create it!

How do I do that you might ask? You do it by creating a Pilot Course of your material. By doing this smaller version of your course, you can then evaluate if you should turn your material into a full course.

When you are doing a BETA launch, you are launching your course at a reduced price just to get students in the door and create good testimonials that you can include in your marketing materials.

To make sure that you are building something that people actually want, listen to your target audience, ask them questions. Normally they will tell you what they want. This can become easier if you have created a following through social media or if you have created an email list. Perhaps you have started a Facebook group in a certain niche market and you already have some followers there.

I believe that for me, this is the next logical step to take to create some courses in my near future. I will be doing it through my mentor who has helped me with this book. He will definitely teach you How to Monetize Your Skills! This is his link if you want to take a look at what he does and how he can help you. www.profitchic.com/chance

Figuring out your Target Audience

Who do you want to serve? Who is your target audience? Do you know where your target audience hangs out online? You can start out by hanging out on social media where your audience hangs out. It might be Facebook, Instagram, LinkedIn, listen to what they are saying in their comments. What are their concerns? Perhaps there are blogs that your audience likes and comments on? Where does your audience interact with the experts in your field? Listen closely to the problems that they are facing. Pay attention to their Interest and topics. You will surely read on what they think that is wrong, or on something that they can't figure out.

You might start seeing patterns emerging. When you identify these patterns, take note of them. You might just have uncovered a problem that your audience wants you to fix! NOW is your opportunity to offer a solution they will pay for.

Making Your First Sale

Do some research online to figure out the pricing on the course you have created. Do a pricing comparison and check the price ranges of comparable courses? After comparing, choose the price range of your course.

Now you are going to create a Landing Page. This is a small one page where you are going to present your pre-sale offer. These can be created with an easy to use software that I had mentioned earlier in the previous Affiliate Chapter. But you can go here, www.theprofitchic.com/osp to access it.

After creating this Landing Page for your course, one of the best ways to get this offer in front of a large audience, is by writing a guest post on a blog. Go back to where your audience hangs out, and where you first discovered the issues they were having. When you write this post, include your link in the by-line. This link, is the link to your Landing page. This Landing Page needs to catch their eye. It will pique their curiosity and will make them want some more information on what you have to offer. When your audience clicks on this link, it will them take them to an Opt-In page, and it's in this page where you will collect their name and email address so you can contact them. Then, they can find out more about you, and what you do.

Then you can follow with a series of emails, to convert your leads into customers. In these email series you can include the story behind the course creation and some key details about the course like the material you will be covering, the structure of the course, and the price range. Look in Chapter 5, the E-mail marketing chapter, to refresh your memory on this subject.

You can open registration for your course with a certain number of spots, keeping in mind how many you would want to start off with, and then close your registration for the pilot course.

Where to Get Your Customers

If you have not started to grow your email list, this is something you can start working on before you create your course. This is one of your most valuable assets. Always make sure that you are nurturing those relationships by giving them lots of value, which basically means that while you are cultivating those relationships, you are providing them with some free information and tools. Tell me....what is better than having a warm market of people that already believes in you and trusts enough in you to buy from you?

Facebook is also a great place to find your customers; normally they will be your most loyal audience, those that follow you. It can be through different groups. You can also run some advertising through Facebook to reach your ideal customer. Paid traffic should also be part of your marketing with other social media platforms as well like Instagram, Snapchat, Pinterest and LinkedIn, Twitter, just to name a few. It is key to learn marketing skills for any business as this can make or break your business. If you have a budget to allocate for marketing that is awesome! But if not, that is OK: it just means that we have to learn to do it ourselves. I like to learn regardless whether I pay someone to do it or I do it myself. I prefer having the knowledge. I don't have to know it all, but I do like to have a basic knowledge of how things work. But that's just me!

Well there you GO … Go ahead. Get CREATING!

CHAPTER FOUR
E-BOOKS

Creating e-books are also a good way of making money online. A lot of people make their living this way. Nowadays you can even find kids creating eBooks and selling them on Amazon and different platforms.

When I first came across this information online, my thought was, *Yeah. I can see myself doing this. I love to read, and I love self-help books!* I figured that I could start there on creating my online laptop lifestyle and create some passive income online this way. I actually thought that I would create a series of books, not only in the how to make money online niche market, or internet marketing business, but also on other topics, like relationships. I actually have made a list of book titles that I thought I could start with, and hopefully you will find them sometime soon on Amazon Kindle. I love the idea of doing the work once, when creating the book, and getting paid for it over and over again as people purchase it. I could be making money while I sleep, which is the kind of money I like to make!

For you, perhaps you can create some of these e-books talking about what your passion is, or maybe you have some expertise on a certain subject. Let's say you are into health. Perhaps you are a trainer and you own a gym. You could create an e-book on tips on how you can lose weight in 30 days. Not only could you sell this e-book, but that would also be a great idea for marketing your business. You already have a client base that would probably be interested in purchasing your book. But not only that, perhaps you would generate more business for your personal training sessions and gym memberships. Always be looking for a way to make a profit! Yup.

How much could you possibly make? Well, who knows? A lot of variables would come into play here, from the title of the book (about which they say that if you have a good title you're half way there) to the marketing of the book, and to many other things that could make it a best seller. Some people have done it very successfully. Some people have had movies created from their e-book. But whatever you make is money that you didn't have in the first place, right? And in the long run, it is also a marketing tool if you have a business whether online or offline. And if you don't, you can create an income stream just writing these books. They are actually not very long at all. They can be anywhere from 30 to100 pages long.

Now, in any venture you can either do it the easy way or the hard way. The easiest way would be to buy a course from someone that has already done it or that specializes in that. It would be like when you buy a franchise. When you buy a franchise, the system is in place so that you know step by step what to do and what vendors to use, etc. But sometimes financially that is not possible, and believe me I understand as I have been there! So in that case, it takes longer. And we have to learn by trial and error; which is the hard way. But it is what it is! Don't let that stop you! And don't make excuses! Remember what I said about having a positive mindset. Research as much free information that you can, or purchase other e-books that tell you how to do it step by step and that are inexpensive to buy. I will list a couple of resources here.

What makes a bestselling e-book? According to some experts, it's usually, a well-researched topic.

Here are four steps you need to take:

1. Target your topic
2. Title your book
3. Type the manuscript
4. Take it to market

Find a universal topic. Typically, this is a topic that when you search your particular key words on your topic, you will find out how many people are searching for that particular subject. Go to Google or Yahoo to search how many people are typing in the key words on your particular topic. There are also other tools out there that you can use to do these searches. If you find about 30,000 or 50,000 relevant keyword searches to your topic, then you might have found a good one. And this will justify you writing your e-book. If your topic idea is unique enough, it might be able to compete with the information that is out there on your particular subject.

Make sure that the information you are putting out there is not easily found as free content or on other e-books. The harder it is to find information on your subject, the less competition there is, and the better off you will be. A minimum of 20,000- 30,000 searches on the keyword relevant to your book, can justify writing the e-book.

Here are some sources for you where you can get a book or e-book published:

This source is an e-book that will give you step-by-step instructions and resources to creating your e-books. http://07e83lyiudv2nbe9s-dkr2cs3f.hop.clickbank.net/?tid=CREATINGE-BOOKS

This guide is a link that will help you to self-publish http://getmyguide.xulonpress.com/xulon-press/?gclid=CLPj_unEn-9QCFVeewAod8bAF6g

Once you have created your e-book(s),

you will have created a sales machine on autopilot. Hell Yeah! This sales machine, will work for you 24 hours a day, 365 days a week. Talking about leveraging your time and making money while you sleep!

That's the whole reason why I left my JOB (**Just Over Broke**) in the first place!

Yes, Sir, staying at home and working as much as I want, whenever I want, is much more rewarding! You just need to have the determination to make it happen!

Just make sure you get self-education on the subject. That is the reason why I quote Jim Rohn who said, and I will quote again.

"Formal Education will make you a living; self-education will make you a fortune."

CHAPTER FIVE
EMAIL MARKETING

Email marketing deserves its own chapter. Not only because this is a way to make money online, but because this is something that you can incorporate as a marketing strategy for whatever business you decide to start online. I want to explain in more detail how email marketing can be used.

Basically, an email list is a list of individuals. You don't just add email addresses of people you may know; anyone can do that. This can lead to people just ignoring your emails or marking them as spam! These are people that have signed up to receive info from you.

It is important that you use a service provider that is reputable to create your list. Through these platforms of providers, you have access to a range of statistics to your emails. Not only that, but there are certain rules to follow with anti-spam laws, and they make sure you are in compliance and that you are building your list correctly.

Here are some of the companies that provide these services. They have different packages that range from free for a certain amount of subscribers, to a 30-day free trial and starting at about $20.00 a month for about 500 subscribers. Keep in mind that as your list grows, so does the price.

Email Marketing Service Providers

1. Aweber
2. MailChimp
3. Constant Contact

I recommend that you spend some time reviewing and comparing these service providers before you make a decision which one suits your business needs better. These are only a few companies. There are many more.

Why Is Building an Email List Important?

The main reason why building your email list is important is because you have control over it. You own it and you control it. Look at it this way: if you relied mostly on social media to generate customers, and all of a sudden they make changes, like Facebook is constantly doing; that is something out of your control. Like the way they are doing now, to get you to pay to boost your posts, they are now controlling who sees your post. This way you can choose how much contact you wish to have with your list; and how many offers you want to make to your lists. You can create different lists, which are basically groups of people. This is going to depend on what products you want to sell or promote. You want to break down your lists by niches so you can promote products that are relevant to that group of people. You can then do different marketing campaigns for different offers to see which ones work best. Unless you choose to stay only with one particular niche. Either way the most powerful way to reach someone, is still through their inbox.

Growing Your List

OK. So now you have chosen your provider to host your list-building. You now need to create an Opt-In Form (short and simple small page where you will ask for their email address). You can create these through their platform or you can use a software, which is what I prefer, because I can create as many as I want and I can test different ones to see which one works better? These are the ones I recommend www.theprofitchic.com/osp or www.theprofitchic.com/clickfunnels.

Remember, just as when creating an e-book all these thing are important when creating an Opt-In page. From the colors to the font to the phrases you use, you want to create something that will catch their eye and will compel them to give you their information. The simpler the better. Every extra piece of information you request from them, diminishes the possibilities of you getting their email address. Their name and email address is basically all you will need. You may also want to include a line saying something like this "I will never spam you or sell your address to anyone else"; this will make your reader feel safer to sign up.

Normally marketers will offer an incentive to get them to sign up. Usually it's an e-book or a PDF Report of some sort. But, if you want to be a little different, you could perhaps offer your new subscribers a short sequence of videos that will show them how to go through a particular process.

You can do a sequence of emails for a couple of weeks using these short video trainings. This way they know they are coming, and you get them used to opening your emails. You can automate this with an Autoresponder (a program that automatically generates a set response to all messages sent to a particular email address) which comes with the service of your email service provider.

After creating an Opt-In Page, you want to create a Landing page. This page would be the page they would be landing at after giving you their email address. This page will also be simple and can also be created with the same software that you used to create your Opt-In page (this was the software recommended previously www.theprofitchic.com/osp.

This Landing Page will have the information on the incentive that you are offering them. And let them know what to expect, like weekly tips or newsletters, etc.

Since you will be competing with perhaps hundreds of other emails, it is vital that the content in your email be truly valuable to your reader.

You want to make sure your email gets opened and not ignored. How you title your subject on the email is important to grab their attention to make them want to open your email. The HOW TO posts are always popular. So if your subject line suggests help with their concern or problem, they are much more likely to open your email.

Ways to Make Money from Your Email List

You can promote your own product, or someone else's if you decide to do Affiliate marketing. Remember the first chapter? This is where you get affiliated with different companies through a platform where you can sell other people's products/service. When promoting other people's products, you will be earning a commission, and that percentage will depend on the product you pick. You want to match your products/services to your audience needs. To feel good about the products you are endorsing, make sure you like or use the product that you are promoting.

You can also make money selling advertising in your emails. Companies will pay money for you to include their information on your emails, just as they do to advertise on websites. However, this is usually when you have a big list of people to email. But a word of caution here, be careful not to over-pack your emails with ads, because you don't want that many people unsubscribing.

Common Mistakes

We all make mistakes, especially at the beginning when we are first starting out. Here are some common mistakes that you want to avoid. You need to decide on a mailing schedule and stick to it! If you decide to do it weekly, then do it. You don't want to start weekly and then life happens and months go by and you don't email your list, especially if you promised to be emailing them weekly. This can easily annoy your subscribers. If you want to do some changes, do it gradually.

Don't be afraid to ask your readers to forward your emails to friends. Just as we ask them to LIKE our Facebook pages, encourage them to forward the information to their friends if they found the information useful.

Some of your readers may unsubscribe when sending an email to your list. Don't let this upset you! Don't take it personally. Some people will clean their inbox. Look at it this way: you will no longer be paying to have them on your list, especially if they were not going to buy from you to begin with.

How to grow your list

There a several ways to grow your list. You can do so by using the Opt-In pages I talked about earlier.

Facebook Ads. You can run super targeted ads that can bring the right people to your product.

Facebook Fan Pages. Starting a Facebook group can also help you grow your audience and convert them into subscribers.

YouTube. Advertising is another source for generating traffic. You can find the right target audience to build your list.

Digital Publishing. Publishing new information or products can generate new subscribers.

Solo Ads. This concept is basically, two marketers swapping email promotions and helping each other build their list. You can also purchase these.

Ok, so now you have decided to start making money through email marketing. Here you get a glimpse of how doing this works. If you decided this is for you, then I would suggest that you immerse yourself into learning more in detail how this process works.

There are different processes you can follow on how you will generate leads to grow your lists. This is where your marketing skills will kick in! Remember that the internet is always changing, so it's important to stay up to speed on the changes and tools that are out there.

Email marketing is going to work, no matter what business you decide to pursue online!

CONCLUSION

I remember feeling overwhelmed, when I first started this journey of making money online. There's an overwhelming amount of information out there. So overwhelming, that it can paralyze you in your journey. Have you heard of Paralysis by Analysis? Yeah…. that was definitely me, LOL.

It's my biggest hope that this book will shed some light for you, and give you some insight of the opportunities that exist out there. Hopefully, it will give you a starting point. Start with one opportunity, and master it, until you become an expert at it. Then you can expand into other ways of making money online. For me, it's important to build multiple streams of income.

I don't know about you, but I am done with building someone else's dream and working for someone else. I am soooooo done with living paycheck to paycheck and defiantly done with the feast or famine routine! Ugh!

The biggest reason for me pursuing an online business, was because of the TIME FREEDOM. I want to be able to have a flexible schedule and spend time with the people I love!

Another piece of advice I can give you is never stop learning and growing in knowledge. Always keep improving yourself. Seek WISDOM like gold! Don't be afraid to take a risk and try new things. Implement what you have learned.

Set up small goals and take one step at a time so it becomes more achievable, so you don't get overwhelmed, but always taking into account what your BIG TIME GOAL is. Well, now you have a starting point. Pay attention to which of these ways of making money you are attracted to, and follow your dreams. It is my deepest desire to Encourage, Empower, and Equip you to live a better life! You are never at your peak! So never stop learning!

Thank you so much for reading this book!

To your Success,

Erika Nino
"The Profit Chic"
www.theprofitchic.com

ACKNOWLEDGMENTS

First of all, I would like to Thank GOD for His wisdom and revelation. And for giving me the ability to start from scratch! And also for his connections, and divine appointments. Which all come into play into my destiny.

You are part of who I am, and without you this would not be possible. Thank you for answering my prayers from years ago when I shared with you that I would like to write some books. And thank you for parting "The Red Sea" for me many times over, when I didn't see a way out!

I would also like to thank my husband Michael Nino, for supporting me in all my Business ventures and not giving up on me. Love you, Babe!

To my son Kole Michael Nino, I want to inspire you to keep reaching for the stars and explore the talents God has given you. I believe in you, more than words can say!

And foremost, a great big Thank You to Randrick Chance, for inspiring, encouraging and mentoring me to write this book. This would not have been possible without your help and your *Monetize Your Skills Academy* course.

ABOUT THE AUTHOR

Hello friends. My name is Erika Nino, and I come from a Financial Service background, teaching others how to prepare for retirement and increase and protect their wealth. I also have a background working in Human Resources. I have been a business owner, owning a Consignment shop and manufacturing swimwear for wholesale.

I remember growing up … I lived next door to an older lady that had a little convenience store next to our house. I would go visit her and play STORE, pretending to own my own store. So I guess Entrepreneurship is in my blood.

The last job I had in the Financial Industry made me realize that I was building someone else's dream. I hated every minute of it in the short time that I was working there. That point is when I decided that life was wayyyyyyy tooooooooo short to be living life by default and stressing out in a job with a company that I despised.

So, I decided to pursue the journey to create the life style I have always wanted to live: a life of time freedom, a life of multiple streams of income, a life of making money while I sleep.

But ... where do I start? In this book, you will find several different ways you can make money online.

To Your Success,
Erika Nino

RESOURCES

Are you Leaving Money On The Table?

Monetize Your Skills Academy (MYSA) *is* the ultimate 6-Figure blueprint that reveals how to turn your education, expertise, and experiences into a 6-figure+ income.

Enroll now in **Monetize Your Skills Academy** (MYSA) and access the secret system to:

- Make a lasting impact.
- Fund your dreams.
- Become Debt-free.
- Sustain your mission, message, or cause.

Go to www.TheProfitChic.com/chance and let's get started today. See you on the inside!

Disclaimer:

The information that is contained within this book is designed to entertain and educate you on my journey. It will give you different ideas of ways you can make money online. Erika Nino aka "The Profit Chic" or Red Sea Media, LLC, makes no promises or guarantees of any income or earnings. Neither Erika Nino nor Red Sea Media, LLC, will be held liable for any losses due to implementing any of the ideas contain in this book.

Do your own due diligence if you are considering changing careers or pursuing starting a business online. You may or may NOT make any money. Monetary and income results will depend on your work ethic, your skills and your practices. Starting any business is a risk, and it may or may NOT be profitable.

Erika Nino aka "The Profit Chic" is affiliated to some of the companies recommended in this book. If you choose to purchase some of these services through her links, she will be compensated by receiving a commission. In which case, she greatly appreciates your support. Thank you.

CREDITS

Bio photo credit

https://www.facebook.com/
Guajardos-gallery-photography
-184170945053862/

Courtesy

www.Guajardogalleryphotography.com.

www.ingramcontent.com/pod-product-compliance
Lightning Source LLC
Chambersburg PA
CBHW030908180526
45163CB00004B/1759